Henry

A Shakespeare Story

RETOLD BY ANDREW MATTHEWS
ILLUSTRATED BY TONY ROSS

ORCHARD

For Marc
A.M.

For Kate and Jason
T.R.

ORCHARD BOOKS
338 Euston Road, London NW1 3BH
Orchard Books Australia
Hachette Children's Books
Level 17/207 Kent St, Sydney, NSW 2000
This text was first published in Great Britain in the form of a gift collection
called The Orchard Book of Shakespeare Stories, illustrated by
Angela Barrett in 2001.
This edition first published in hardback in Great Britain in 2002
First paperback publication in 2003
This slipcase edition published in 2013
Not for individual resale
Text © Andrew Matthews 2001
Illustrations © Tony Ross 2002
ISBN 978 1 40780 986 1
The rights of Andrew Matthews to be identified as the author and Tony Ross as
the illustrator of this work have been asserted by them in accordance with the
Copyright, Designs and Patents Act, 1988
A CIP catalogue record for this book is available from the British Library
Printed in China

Orchard Books is a division of Hachette Childrens Books,
an Hachette UK company.
www.hachette.co.uk

Contents

Cast List

King Henry V

Duke of Exeter
Uncle to the King

Earl of Cambridge
A conspirator against the King

Michael Williams

A soldier in the King's army

A French ambassador

A French messenger

The Scene

England and France in the fifteenth century.

I see you stand like greyhounds in the slips,
Straining upon the start. The game's afoot.
Follow your spirit, and upon this charge
Cry, 'God for Harry! England and Saint George!'

King Henry; III.i.

Henry V

Hardly anyone called the new King 'Henry'. When they talked about him they said 'Hal' or 'Harry', or used one of his other nicknames. Everyone knew what a wild and rebellious teenager the young prince had been.

Harry had spent more time with rascally old Sir John Falstaff, learning how to drink and gamble than he had with his  royal father. Now the reckless young Harry was King, but no one knew what sort of king he would be. Some thought he would be a disaster, others said that only time would tell, but all were aware that the young King faced a difficult time as the new English monarch.

England and France had been at war for twenty-five years, and though the two countries had agreed a truce, the truce was an uneasy one. A weak English king who didn't have the support of his people might give the French just the chance they wanted to carry out a successful invasion...

One morning, not long after Henry's coronation, the nobles of the High Council were gathered together in the Reception Chamber of the King's palace in London. Among them was the Duke of Exeter, the King's uncle. He knew that Henry was now about to face his most challenging test. 'How young and lonely he looks on that great throne,' Exeter thought. 'He has his mother's dark hair and soft eyes – but does he have any of his father's courage, I wonder?'

His question was soon answered, for just then the doors of the great chamber opened and an ambassador from the Dauphin, the Crown Prince of France, entered. The ambassador was a perfumed dandy with his curled beard, and the clothes he wore were as brightly-coloured as a peacock's feathers. Behind him, two guards carried a large wooden chest which they set down on the floor.

The ambassador gave an elaborate bow. "Your Highness," he said, in a voice as smooth as honey. "My master, the Dauphin, sends greetings."

"I want more than greetings," Henry replied coldly. "I asked King Charles to give me back the French lands that my father won from him. What is his answer?"

The ambassador ran his fingers through the curls of his beard and smirked. "The King is busy with important matters," he said. "His Majesty thought that since the Dauphin is closer to you in age, it would be better for him to deal with your request."

Henry felt a sting of anger at the ambassador's insolent tone, but he kept his voice calm. "And what is the Dauphin's message?" he asked.

"The Dauphin thinks you are a little too young to bother yourself with affairs of state," said the ambassador, gesturing towards the wooden chest. "So he has sent a present which he thinks will be more suitable than the right to French dukedoms."

The ambassador clicked his fingers
and the guards opened the lid of the
chest. It was filled with tennis balls. One
of them fell out and rolled to the foot of
Henry's throne.

The nobles glanced at each other anxiously. King Henry had been insulted and humiliated in front of all his courtiers. How would he respond?

Henry leaned over and picked up the ball at his feet. He bounced it once, and caught it in his right hand. "Tell the Dauphin that he has begun a game with me that he'll wish he had never started,"

he said. "His mockery will turn these tennis balls into cannon balls! The people of France may be laughing at the Dauphin's joke, but they'll weep before I'm finished!"

The ambassador's face went deathly pale. He bowed low and left the chamber. When the door closed behind him, the nobles began  to talk among themselves. Most of them glanced admiringly at Henry, but the Earl of Cambridge scowled at the King. He raised his voice above the hubbub in the chamber and said, "Your Majesty spoke hastily. You should have sought the advice of older and wiser men before plunging our country into war."

"An insult to me is an insult to the English people!" Henry snapped. "And besides, my lord Cambridge, I don't listen to the advice of traitors!"

Cambridge started as though someone had jabbed him with a knife point and his eyes bulged with fear.

"You thought that because of my youth, I could easily be deceived," Henry went on, "but I've found you out. You betrayed your country for French gold and worked as a spy for King Charles. Guards, take him to the Tower!"

The nobles stared in astonishment at the disclosure of Cambridge's treachery and at seeing the determination of their young King. He was wiser and stronger-minded than any of them had realised.

Men from all over the country answered the young King's call to war with France.

Blacksmiths,

farm-workers,

wheelwrights,
weavers and clerks...

...all left their homes and marched along
the roads that led to Southampton.

The younger men thought that war would be a kind of holiday and were eager for fame and glory; others, who had fought before and knew what battle was like, were grim-faced and silent.

At Southampton, the men began their training. Hour after hour and day after day they marched and drilled. At the archery butts men with longbows practised until their aim was true.

Slowly, the raggle-taggle band of
volunteers was transformed into an
army. When all was ready, the English
battle fleet set sail for the French port
of Harfleur.

*** *** ***

It took all day for Henry's men to cross the Channel and unload the ships. The men spent the night on the beach and were woken in the grey hours before

dawn to sharpen their weapons and make ready their siege-ladders and battering-rams. On the skyline the walls of Harfleur looked like an ominous cloud.

When the sun rose, Henry rode out
in front of his men on his dapple-grey
war-horse, the early morning light glinting
on his armour. "The English are a
peaceful nation," he told the troops, "but
when war comes, we can fight like tigers!
Let the light of battle blaze in your eyes,
to burn the courage of your enemies! Let
your cry be: *God for Harry, England and
St George!*"

Cannons roared like a gigantic wave breaking on the shore as the English army charged. By nightfall, Harfleur had fallen.

* * *

Henry was planning to advance to the port of Calais, which was already in English possession. The next morning a messenger arrived from King Charles.

"The King commands that you surrender to him and leave France while you still can!" the messenger declared scornfully. "He is camped at Agincourt with an army of fifty thousand. If you do not agree to his terms, he will advance and crush you!"

"Your Majesty!" the Duke of Exeter murmured. "We only have four thousand men. If the French attack us here, all will be lost!"

"Then we must go to them, Uncle," Henry said calmly. He turned to the messenger. "Tell King Charles that his army is in my way," he said. "I will march to Agincourt and, if he does not step aside, the earth will be red with French blood!"

And so the English advanced to Agincourt
and set up camp facing the French, on
a plain between two woods. When the
French saw the size of the English army
they whistled and jeered, beating their
swords against their shields to make a
great clamour.

But Henry shut his ears to their taunts and concentrated on positioning his forces. He discussed battle plans with his commanders late into 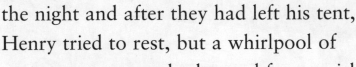 the night and after they had left his tent, Henry tried to rest, but a whirlpool of doubts and fears swirled in his mind, and he could not sleep. Hoping to calm himself, he put on a hooded cloak and went walking through the camp.

Men lay asleep, huddled around fires.
The air was filled with the sound of snores,
or voices shouting out in terror through
nightmares. Across the plain glimmered the
fires of the French camp, as numberless as
the stars on a winter's night.

Henry was so deep in thought that he didn't notice a sentry on guard beside one camp fire until he almost walked on to the point of the man's spear.

"Who goes there?" barked the sentry.

"A friend," Henry replied.

"Who is your commander?"

"The Duke of Exeter."

The guard lowered his spear and pulled a face. "A fine soldier!" he grunted. "If he were leading the army instead of the King, we wouldn't be in this mess. I bet young Harry wishes he was back in London, tucked up safe in bed."

"The King wishes himself nowhere but here," said Henry.

The guard turned his head to spit into the fire. Light from the flames played across his broken nose and the long scar on his left cheek.

"Kings!" he growled. "They do the arguing, but it's the likes of you and me who do the fighting and the dying!"

"Tomorrow the King will fight in the front line, alongside his men, you will see," said Henry.

"I'll wager a week's wages that he'll be at the back, with a fast horse ready for his escape!" the guard said bitterly.

"Very well," said Henry. "If we both survive, find me when the battle's over and we'll see who was right. What's your name?"

"Michael Williams," said the guard. "What's yours?"

"Harry le Roy," Henry said with a smile, then he passed on and disappeared into the darkness.

* * *

In the early hours of the morning a thunderstorm broke. Rain fell mercilessly, drenching English and French alike and turning the plain into a sea of mud. The rain stopped just before dawn, but the sky was still filled with heavy black clouds.

The first line
of the French
army took
the field, led
by knights on
horseback.
The plumes
on their helmets
fluttered brightly
against the dark sky, and their armour
shone like silver. Behind them
ran infantrymen in chain-mail
coats, carrying blue
shields painted with
golden fleurs-de-lis.

Henry ordered his
archers to stand
ready and wait for
his signal.

The French knights broke into a gallop.
The hooves of the horses shook the
ground, and spattered their riders with
mud. The knights lowered their lances
and screamed out a battle cry, but
halfway to the English line, the French

horses ran into boggy ground and the
charge faltered. The knights pulled at their
reins in panic, turning their horses to try
and find firmer footing. The infantrymen
caught up, and all was a surging chaos of
whinnying horses and cursing men.

Henry drew his
sword and swept
it high above his
head. "Fire!"
he bellowed.

At his command,
a thousand arrows
left a thousand
longbows and made a
sound like the wind sighing through the
boughs of a forest. A deadly hail struck the
French, piercing armour,
and flesh, and bone.
Knights fell from
their saddles and
startled horses
bolted, trampling
anyone who stood
in their way.

Volley after volley of arrows whistled down, until the only movement on the battlefield came from the wounded as they attempted to crawl back to safety.

A second line of French troops charged.
Once more the English archers stopped
them. The French tried to retreat, but ran

into their own third line as it came up
behind them. It was then that Henry led
his men in a charge. The two armies met
with a clash like a clap of thunder.

The fighting
lasted for two
hours.
The French
soldiers, dismayed
and confused,
found that their
commanders had been
killed and there was no
one to give them orders. They fought

bravely, but the
fury of the
English attack
proved too
much for
them, and
at last they
broke ranks
and fled.

Seven thousand Frenchmen died at Agincourt, including many great noblemen. The English lost only a hundred men.

* * *

That night, at sunset, a French messenger
rode into the English camp carrying a
white flag of truce. It was the same man
who had come to Harfleur, but this time he
was not haughty. His armour was dented
and there was dirt and blood on his face.

"King Charles begs for peace," he said humbly. "He will return all the lands that you claim and he asks you to accept the hand of his daughter, Princess Catherine, so that your two families may be united in peace forever."

"Tell the King that I accept," said Henry. "We will meet, and draw up a peace treaty."

53

That night, there were celebrations in
the English camp and just before midnight,
Henry slipped away from his commanders
and went in search of Michael Williams.
He found him at the same guard point as
on the previous night.

When Williams saw Henry, he dropped to one knee. "Your Majesty," he mumbled. "I did not know who you were last night, but I recognised you today when you led the charge."

"So," said Henry, smiling. "I won the wager."

"I was a fool to speak the way I did last night!" said the sentry apologetically.

Henry put his hand on the man's
shoulder and took a bag of gold coins
from his belt. He handed it to the
astonished guard.

"Here," Henry said. "You spoke your
mind last night. I hope that honest men will
always speak to me as openly as you did."

✳ ✳ ✳

So King Henry the Fifth won a famous
victory – and more importantly, he won
the hearts of all his subjects. Now they
respected him as a ruler, but they also
loved him because he understood the lives
of ordinary people, and was always ready
to listen to them.

And he won more than his subjects'
hearts, for when he met Catherine, the
French princess, they fell in love at once –
even though she could not speak English
and his clumsy French made her laugh.
With their marriage, the bitter war with
France was ended in feasting and
friendship.

This star of England. Fortune made his sword,
By which the world's best garden he achieved,

Chorus; V.ii.

Patriotism in Henry V

There were no newspapers, radio or television in Shakespeare's time, so it is difficult to know what ordinary people thought about what was happening in the world around them. However, dramatists often reflected popular opinions in their plays, and *Henry V* is an example of this.

Shakespeare wrote the play in 1599, the same year that the Earl of Essex led an army to put down a rising in Ireland. Many hoped that Essex would win as famous a victory as Henry V at Agincourt.

The play is based on historical events, but Shakespeare shapes the facts to present a picture of a country uniting under a strong leader to face a fearsome enemy. The rousing, patriotic speeches in the play capture the patriotic mood of

Elizabethan England.

In *Henry V*, no one expects Henry to be a good king because of his wild behaviour as a prince. But once on the throne, he displays wisdom and courage.

On the night before the battle of Agincourt, Henry, disguised as an ordinary foot soldier, has a conversation with a sentry. Shakespeare presents a leader who is not distant from his people. This is a king in touch with his subjects, and one who values their honesty.

In the battle that follows, huge numbers of the French army are killed, while only a few Englishmen lose their lives. The audience, cheering the actors at the end of the performance, would also have been expressing their patriotism and pride in their country and its achievements.

Shakespeare and the Globe Theatre

Some of Shakespeare's most famous plays were first performed at the Globe Theatre, which was built on the South Bank of the River Thames in 1599.

Going to the Globe was a different experience from going to the theatre today. The building was roughly circular in shape, but with flat sides: a little like a doughnut crossed with a fifty-pence piece. Because the Globe was an open-air theatre, plays were only put on during daylight hours in spring and summer. People paid a penny to stand in the central space and watch a play, and this part of the audience became known as 'the groundlings' because they stood on the ground. A place in the tiers of seating beneath the thatched roof, where there was a slightly better view and less chance of being rained on, cost extra.

The Elizabethans did not bath very often and the audiences at the Globe were smelly. Fine ladies and gentlemen in the more expensive seats sniffed perfume and bags of sweetly-scented herbs to cover the stink rising from the groundlings.

There were no actresses on the stage; all the female characters in Shakespeare's plays would have been acted by boys, wearing wigs and make-up. Audiences were not well-behaved. People clapped and cheered when their favourite actors came on stage; bad actors were jeered at and sometimes pelted with whatever came to hand.

Most Londoners worked hard to make a living and in their precious free time they liked to be entertained. Shakespeare understood the magic of the theatre so well that today, almost four hundred years after his death, his plays still cast a spell over the thousands of people that go to see them.

Orchard Classics
Shakespeare Stories

RETOLD BY ANDREW MATTHEWS
ILLUSTRATED BY TONY ROSS

Orchard Books are available from all good bookshops.